MASTER YOUR MIND

MASTER YOUR MIND

The Student-Athlete's Blueprint for Mental Toughness & Elite Performance

Tyler Ganus

Published by Game Changer Publishing

Paperback ISBN: 978-1-968250-73-7

Hardcover ISBN: 978-1-968250-72-0

Digital ISBN: 978-1-968250-74-4

GC GAME CHANGER
PUBLISHING
www.GameChangerPublishing.com

FROM THE EXPERTS

"He is a living legend. What he has inside of his heart is a tremendous work ethic. The kid is just unbelievable. He's such a person you can root for. You kinda tear up when you talk about Tyler Ganus because nobody works as hard as him as I've ever coached in my life."

— Mark Wasikowski,
Head Baseball Coach of the Oregon Ducks

"One of my favorite people I've ever had the chance to coach and just be around in general. Ganus has a rare gift most people don't. We talk about him all the time as the standard for doing things the right way. No matter what he achieves on the field, his legacy is already secure because of who he is off of it. He could win the Golden Spikes Award, and it still wouldn't top the kind of person he is."

— Marcus Hinkle,
Assistant Baseball Coach of the Oregon Ducks

"He listens, he asks questions. He's a really effective leader because he lives it every day. He treats people the right way, has great perspective, and cares about his teammates."

— Ben Greenspan,
Head Baseball Coach of the Northwestern Wildcats

"He stands for all the right things. He puts his head down, works hard, grits his teeth, and pushes through adversity. He understands he's not perfect and is always looking for ways to learn and grow. But when he's in the box, on base, or in the outfield—he carries a confidence and swagger that says he's going to make a play."

— Ben Keizer,
Pitching Coach of the Northwestern Wildcats

READ THIS FIRST

Just to say thanks for buying and reading my book!

Scan the QR Code for a free
one-on-one coaching call!

MASTER YOUR MIND

The Student-Athlete's Blueprint for Mental Toughness & Elite Performance

TYLER GANUS

PREFACE

This book is more than words on a page—
it's a piece of my heart, my journey, and my belief in you.

This book—and the entire **Collegiate Mind Mastery** movement—was born from the desire to give back. To offer the kind of guidance I wish I had during the hardest moments of my athletic and academic journey. Whether you're facing setbacks, chasing a dream, or trying to figure out where you fit into this world, this book is for you.

It's for the athlete who wakes up early to train before school.

The one who studies late after practice.

The one who feels unseen but shows up anyway.

The one who refuses to quit.

You don't need to be the most talented. But you do need to be consistent. You need to think differently. Move intentionally. And most of all, believe in yourself, especially on the days it's hardest to do so.

I believe every athlete has the power to level up—mentally, physically, and emotionally—and go get what they truly deserve. But it starts in the mind. **Champions aren't born. They're built**. And they're built from the inside out.

This book is a call to action for every student-athlete ready to grow, lead, and live purposefully. It's broken into sections you can return to again and again. Use it during your season. Use it during the offseason. Use it when you feel stuck or fired up.

The lessons here aren't theory. They're real. They're lived. And they're meant to help you become the strongest version of yourself.

Let's get to work.

– *Tyler Ganus*

CONTENTS

Part 4
PERSPECTIVE, GRATITUDE, AND GROWTH

INTRODUCTION

For the Reader

Before we dive into the strategies, stories, and mindset tools in this book, I want to make something clear:

This book isn't just something you read—it's something you *do*.

You'll find four key sections designed to help you unlock your potential:

1. **The Foundation of Mental Toughness**: Building self-belief, grit, and emotional strength.
2. **Championship Habits & A Daily Edge**: Creating routines and behaviors that separate you from your opponents.
3. **Success Leaves Clues**: Insights from top athletes, coaches, and elite performers.

4. **Perspective, Gratitude, and Growth**: Keeping your purpose at the center of the grind.

Throughout the book, you'll come across reflections, journal prompts, and action steps. Take them seriously. *The athletes who grow the most are the ones who take what they learn and apply it daily.*

If you're reading this, you're likely the kind of person who wants more. More growth. More clarity. More purpose. This book is for you. Whether you're an underclassman trying to find your confidence, a college player aiming to lead, or just someone hungry to level up, my goal is to help you build a mindset that wins both on and off the field.

My Story

I grew up in Los Angeles and had the honor of representing Team USA at the 12U Pan American Games in Mazatlán, Mexico, where we brought home a silver medal. I pitched in two combined no-hitters during that tournament—memories I'll never forget.

From there, I attended Harvard-Westlake High School and earned a walk-on spot at the University of Oregon. At Oregon, I became part of the 2023 Pac-12 championship team and completed my undergraduate degree in just three years. I then transferred to Northwestern University, where I earned my first Division I scholarship, became an everyday starter, and helped lead the team to its highest win percentage in the last twenty years.

Tyler poses for Northwestern's 2025 media day.
Credit: Mary Grace Grabill, Northwestern Athletics

My story is one of resilience and relentless pursuit. I wasn't a five-star recruit. I was an underdog who outworked the odds. My mindset shaped everything—from earning dual graduate certificates in Sports Communication and Technology Entrepreneurship to graduating summa cum laude with a GPA above 4.0 at both Oregon and Northwestern.

Some of the honors and experiences I'm most proud of include:

- Team USA Silver Medalist
- 2023 Pac-12 Champion & Vanderbilt Regional Champion
- 2023 Rawlings "Big Stick" Batting Title (.345)
- 2025 Big Ten Sportsmanship Award
- 2025 Big Ten Jackie Robinson Community & Impact Award Nominee (Northwestern Campus Winner)
- 2025 Allstate/NACDA Good Works Team Winner
- 2025 Academic All-District Team
- 2025 Academic All-Big 10 Team
- 2025 Pomeranz Family Willie the Wildcat Award
- 2023 Jaqua Award (Highest Student-Athlete GPA at Oregon)
- 6× Dean's List
- B.S. in Music
- Graduate Certificates in Sports Communication & Technology Entrepreneurship

My mission is simple:

Help student-athletes like you grow into mentally tough, self-aware leaders who show up with purpose ... every day.

Let's dive in and build the mindset of a champion.

Part 1

THE FOUNDATION OF MENTAL TOUGHNESS

"You have power over your mind—not outside events.
Realize this, and you will find strength."
– Marcus Aurelius

BE A FOUNTAIN, NOT A DRAIN

One of the most powerful lessons I learned from Brian Cain's *Mental Performance Mastery* program is the idea of being a fountain of energy, not a drain. Your presence affects your team. **Every time you show up with positivity, support, and energy, you're pouring life into your teammates**. On the other hand, when you pout, complain, or let frustration take over, you're draining that same energy from the culture.

Let me give you a quick example. Imagine you just struck out in a big moment. Instead of sulking in the dugout, what if you popped up and started cheering for the next guy? What if your energy fueled him to get the job done?

That's what a fountain does. **A fountain builds culture.** A fountain builds confidence. A fountain is contagious in the best way.

Tyler celebrates with Preston Knott after hitting
a go-ahead homer in the 10th inning to lift
Northwestern over Maryland 6-5.
Credit: Allison Mize, Northwestern Athletics

Being a fountain doesn't mean you fake positivity. It means you lead with strength. You bounce back quickly. You pick others up when they're down. You make eye contact in the dugout or on the sidelines and that can shift the momentum. You clap, lock in, and create momentum with your mindset. And it's contagious—just like negativity. One guy with bad body language can poison a whole bench. But one guy with elite focus and encouragement? That can shift an entire inning.

Practical Ways to Be a Fountain:

- **After a mental mistake**, be the first to clap for the next person. Don't dwell on the mistake. Move on visibly.
- **Celebrate others' success**—even if you're struggling. Leaders don't need the spotlight to shine.
- **Be vocal.** Echo calls, cheer for your teammates, and stay locked in. Energy travels through your voice.
- **Stay engaged.** Study the game. Talk to coaches. Be curious. Don't check out.
- **Reset routines.** Use deep breaths and visual cues to center yourself and stay steady.
- **Be self-aware.** Check your body language, tone, and facial expressions—they speak louder than words.

Key Takeaway:

Choose to add value, not subtract it. The more energy you pour into your teammates, the more resilient, united, and successful your team becomes—and you'll grow in the process.

Reflection Question:

When was the last time you were a drain? How can you flip the switch and become a fountain in your next practice or game?

_____

_____

_____

_____

_____

_____

_____

_____

THE 4 A.M. CHALLENGE

Some of my best memories from college baseball are early mornings with one of my closest teammates—Isaac Ayon—who went on to get drafted by the Los Angeles Dodgers in 2024. We were obsessed with getting better. We challenged each other to do more, be different, and find an edge that others didn't want to find.

In the fall, we made a pact: be asleep by 8 p.m., wake up at 4 a.m., and train together from 4:30 to 6:30 a.m. before team breakfast. That window became our **secret weapon**. The grind brought us closer. It gave us confidence. We knew we were doing things no one else was willing to do.

A signature 4:30 am lift featuring Tyler and Isaac Ayon.

HARD WORK PAYS OFF

One of the most electric moments of my college career was watching my teammate, **Griffin Mills**, break out of a slump in dramatic fashion. Griffin had a rocky start to his freshman season, in and out of the lineup, struggling to find his rhythm. But what no one could deny was how hard he worked. Every day, extra swings off the machine. Always first in, last out.

Then came our game against Maryland. Bottom of the 8th. Two outs. Down one. Runner on first. Griffin steps up.

Boom! **Home run.**

That moment was earned. Not given. And it wasn't just luck—it was the result of consistent, intentional work done behind the scenes.

Hard work won't guarantee you success. **But it will give you more chances to succeed**. The opportunities multiply when your preparation is relentless.

Griffin Mills enters the dugout after hitting
a pinch-hit homer against Maryland.
Credit: Donald Crocker, Northwestern Athletics

Practical Ways to Build Intentional Work:

- Set **one focused goal** for each training session.
- **Film your reps** and review for five minutes daily to spot improvements.
- **Track your extra work** in a notebook—it builds confidence and accountability.
- Schedule a weekly **thirty-minute "deep work" block** to focus on your biggest weakness.

Key Takeaway:

Mindless reps don't move the needle. But intentional effort over time creates game-changing moments.

Reflection Question:

What is one area of your game where you could apply more focused, intentional effort starting today?

_____

_____

_____

_____

_____

_____

_____

_____

_____

CONTROL THE CONTROLLABLES

One of the most freeing realizations in my journey was this: **You can't control everything—but you can control more than you think.**

You can't control the weather. Or a bad call from the umpire or referee. Or how your coach reacts after a game. However, you *can* control your **thoughts**. You can control your **emotions**. You can control your **actions**. And the more you lock in on those, the more consistent you become.

When you focus too much on results (stats, wins, rankings), your mindset rides a rollercoaster of highs and lows. One good game and you're flying. One mistake and you're spiraling. That's not sustainable. But if you focus on *your process*—your routines, your preparation, your mindset—you build stability.

Tyler comes up clutch with a pinch-hit
single against UCLA.
Credit: Oregon Athletics

That's where the acronym A.C.E. comes in:

Attitude. Concentration. Effort.

These are three things no coach, ref, or opponent can take from you. When you master them, you become mentally unshakable.

Elite athletes don't *hope* to feel confident. They *create* confidence by mastering their mind. And it starts with choosing your thoughts, one rep at a time.

Practical Ways to Control the Controllables:

- Start every day by naming **one thing you're grateful for** (to anchor your attitude).
- Use a **reset routine** (like deep breaths or a cue word) when frustration hits.
- Keep a **preparation checklist** for games and practices—do it every time.
- **Journal one win and one area of growth** after each workout or performance.

Key Takeaway:

Where attention goes, energy flows. Instead of draining your energy on things you can't control, fuel what you can influence.

Reflection Question:

What's one thing outside your control that you've been focusing on too much and what can you shift that energy toward instead?

_____

_____

_____

_____

_____

_____

_____

_____

THE MENTAL WEIGHT ROOM

As a kid, I had the chance to meet **Billy Beane**, the legendary GM behind the *Moneyball* movement. One thing he said stuck with me forever: ***"The smartest players are always the most valuable."***

That quote changed the way I saw baseball. It wasn't just about tools or talent—it was about thinking. Seeing the game. Studying. Being aware. And the best place to build that mindset? The classroom.

Too many athletes treat school like a chore. But the classroom is your mental weight room. It's where you learn discipline, focus, and the ability to process complex information under pressure—**the exact traits that show up in your sport.**

After winning a silver medal for Team USA in the
Pan American Games, Tyler had a special
opportunity to meet the legendary GM, Billy Beane.

Being a student of the game starts with being a student, period. When you commit to being locked in mentally during class, you train your brain to stay sharp. You learn how to adapt, how to listen, how to process. All of these skills directly impact how you play when the game speeds up.

Mental reps matter. Smart players anticipate, adjust, and make teammates better. Talent might get you in the door, but your sport-specific IQ and mindset keep you on the field.

Practical Ways to Make Gains in the Mental Weight Room:

- Challenge yourself to **participate at least one time** in every class—it will help you stay locked in and retain the material.
- Before practice, **reflect on what you learned in school** and how it might help your focus or discipline.
- Use a **planner or notes app** to track mental lessons, not just physical reps.
- Study the game like you **study for a test**—ask questions, watch film, take notes.

Key Takeaway:

Your brain is a muscle. The more reps you give it in the classroom, the stronger your game becomes.

Reflection Question:

What's one habit you can build in the classroom that will also make you a better athlete?

_____

_____

_____

_____

_____

_____

_____

_____

Part 2

CHAMPIONSHIP HABITS AND A DAILY EDGE

"We are what we repeatedly do.
Excellence, then, is not an act, but a habit."
– Will Durant (summarizing Aristotle)

A NAMELESS, FACELESS OPPONENT

One of the most powerful philosophies I learned playing college baseball—both at Oregon and Northwestern—was this: **We're not playing a team ... we're playing *the game*.**

Yes, coaches still gave us scouting reports. We studied tendencies and matchups. But come game time, we weren't obsessing over opponents. We were focused on *us*—on playing the game the right way.

Sports are hard, no matter who you are competing against. The more you fixate on the other team, the more you feed fear, overthinking, and pressure. But when you narrow your focus inward—your routines, your team, your approach—the game slows down. That's where confidence lives.

National Anthem before Oregon defeated Vanderbilt 7–6
in Game 2 of the Nashville Regional.
Credit: Oregon Athletics

This becomes even more important during rivalry games or playoffs. Emotions run high. The crowd gets loud. The chirps get personal. But all of that? It's just noise. Noise only has power if you give it your attention.

When we played **Vanderbilt** in the 2023 Nashville Regional, they had multiple future MLB Draft picks, elite facilities, and a storied program. But we didn't show up to play the brand—we showed up to play the game (we went on to not only defeat Vanderbilt but also win their Regional).

The moment you strip away the labels—"top recruit," "underdog," "high stakes"—you free yourself to focus on what actually matters: pitch by pitch, play by play.

The best competitors I've ever faced didn't care who was watching. **They treated every game, every rep, every pitch the same**—as a chance to dominate.

Practical Ways to Clear the Noise:

- Create a **pregame routine** to lock in on *your* process.
- Think of your **internal phrase** to use as a mental reset.
- Incorporate **deep breaths** into your in-game routines.
- Before each game, write down **three things you can control** and choose to focus on them.

Key Takeaway:

Respect your opponent, but never fear them. Execution beats reputation every time.

Reflection Question:

Are you focused on the name across from you or the game in front of you? Why are you thinking that way?

_____

_____

_____

_____

_____

_____

_____

_____

WHAT BREAKS YOU?

One of the most powerful lessons I learned during my time at Northwestern came from our head coach, Ben Greenspan. He shared a message that's stuck with me ever since—one that originated from legendary football coach Nick Saban.

Mental toughness isn't just about being gritty or intense. It's about being unbreakable.

Coach Greenspan challenged us to ask a hard question, one that strips away ego and forces you to look in the mirror: **"What breaks you?"**

Think about that. What truly rattles you? Is it a bad call from the umpire? Sitting on the bench? Making an error in a big spot?

Batting practice before Northwestern's game
against Nebraska.
Credit: Jake Aks, Northwestern Athletics

It's easy to say we're tough—until the game punches us in the mouth. Until adversity hits. Until pressure mounts. But that's when your true mindset shows. And being honest about what affects you most is the first step toward mastering it.

Mental toughness is not the absence of emotion. It's the ability to respond with intention in the face of discomfort. It's choosing calm over chaos, process over panic.

If strikeouts usually get under your skin, challenge yourself to respond differently. Reset between pitches. Use your breath. Talk to yourself like a champion. Give yourself grace—then get back to work. If it's failure that breaks you, reframe it. Failure is feedback. And feedback fuels growth.

It's not about never getting knocked down. **It's about how quickly and powerfully you get back up.**

Practical Ways to Build Mental Toughness:

- Journal about **what truly rattles you**—get specific and honest.
- Practice **reset routines**: deep breaths, focal points, and self-talk.
- Reflect on **failure as feedback**, not judgment.
- Create a personal **"response plan"** that you can use when faced with adversity during your season.

Key Takeaway:

Mental toughness means being unshakable. The most elite athletes aren't perfect—they're just the fastest to reset, refocus, and rise again.

Reflection Question:

What consistently throws you off your game, and how can you train yourself to respond instead of react?

_____

_____

_____

_____

_____

_____

_____

_____

_____

COMMITMENT > FEELINGS

One of my favorite lessons comes from Ole Miss head baseball coach Mike Bianco. In a viral video, he said something that has stuck with me:

*"Once your commitment is greater than your feelings ...
that's when you get results."*

Let that sink in.

That one sentence captures the difference between average and elite athletes.

The truth is that motivation is temporary. Some days you'll wake up feeling fired up and ready to go. Other days, you won't. That's just life. But your commitment? That's a choice. That's what you lean on when your feelings tell you to quit.

Tyler comes home to score the tying run
in the bottom of the 9th against Illinois.
Credit: Caden Greco, Northwestern Athletics

The real separator isn't what you do when everything feels right. It's what you do when it doesn't. When your legs are sore. When your schedule is packed. When no one's watching. That's when consistency is built. That's when your character is revealed.

At my company, **Collegiate Mind Mastery**, one of our core pillars is mastering your ability to **show up regardless of how you feel**. Anybody can grind when they're hyped up ... but champions? Champions show up on the hard days. They choose effort when it's inconvenient. They embrace the work even when it's boring.

That doesn't mean you have to be perfect. It means you must stay consistent. Consistency builds trust with your teammates, your coaches, and most importantly, **yourself**.

You'll always have reasons to take it easy. **It takes what it takes.**

Practical Ways to Build Consistency Over Feelings:

- Set a **non-negotiable daily habit**—even if it's small (ten push-ups, five minutes of mindset work, etc.).
- Create a **"why" statement** (why you play your sport) that you can read when motivation dips.
- **Rate your effort** at the end of each day, not your results.

- Choose **one thing** you'll do this week, *no matter what,* to get closer to your biggest goal.

Key Takeaway:

Commitment means doing what's required even when it's inconvenient, uncomfortable, or unpopular.

Reflection Question:

Where in your life have you been letting feelings win over commitment?

_____

_____

_____

_____

_____

_____

_____

THE SUIT CHALLENGE

During my sophomore year, I read *Winning: The Unforgiving Race to Greatness* and *Relentless: From Good to Great to Unstoppable* by Tim Grover, the mindset coach to Michael Jordan, Kobe Bryant, and other greats. Those books fired me up. After reading them, I had one question in my head (on repeat): *How can I raise my standards?*

That thought lingered in my mind until I decided to act on it. I made a personal challenge: **wear a suit to every class, practice, meeting, and game for one week**. I wanted to physically remind myself that being elite required more than words—it demanded discipline, intention, and presence.

After completing the suit challenge, Tyler jokingly photoshopped himself and his coach, Marcus Hinkle, into a "Tom and Jerry" logo—declaring victory.

At first, it felt a little ridiculous. Then, one of my coaches, Marcus Hinkle, said I wouldn't last the whole fall. That's all I needed to hear. **Challenge accepted**. Every single day that fall, I showed up in a full suit. Some days were uncomfortable, inconvenient, and awkward—and that was the point.

The suit became my armor. It reminded me to carry myself with purpose and integrity. My standard for excellence wasn't just on the field—it was how I lived every hour of the day.

The truth is, **excellence is a choice**—and it's accomplished through the little things.

Practical Ways to Apply This:

- Choose **one discipline** you'll commit to for thirty days—and stick with it.
- Set a **physical reminder** (wristband, journal, etc.) to raise your daily standards.
- Do something uncomfortable each day to **"callus your mind."**

Key Takeaway:

Raising your standards means taking action when others don't—especially when no one is watching.

Reflection Question:

What's one high-level standard you're ready to commit to—and how will you prove it?

_____

_____

_____

_____

_____

_____

_____

_____

_____

LION MODE

One of the most powerful mindset shifts an athlete can make is learning to flip the switch into **aggression mode**. There's a Ben Lionel Scott motivational video (which I love) that talks about the difference between a lion and an elephant—both powerful animals, but one is feared. One is the king. Why?

Mentality.

The lion doesn't hesitate. It doesn't play it safe. It hunts with conviction. That's the energy you need when you step into competition.

Are you in lion mode when the lights come on? Are you attacking the game—or reacting to it?

Before returning to the field for the final rotation of
batting practice, Tyler reminds himself to **"Compete!"**
Credit: Ryan Kuttler, Northwestern Athletics

I challenge you to tap into your **alter ego** when you compete. Become a version of yourself that's fearless, focused, and aggressive. Swagger matters. Body language matters. Belief matters. You don't need to fake confidence—you need to *choose* it. Every single day.

Aggression doesn't mean recklessness. It means decisive. It means commanding the moment and refusing to play small. You've put in the work. Now act like it.

Practical Ways to Activate Your "Lion Mode":

- Develop a game-day **alter ego** or nickname that represents your fiercest self.
- Practice walking with **confident body language**— head up, chest out, eyes locked in.
- Use an **aggressive trigger** phrase before each rep or play (e.g., "I'm the hunter").
- **Visualize** dominating the competition the night before you compete.

Key Takeaway:

Aggression isn't recklessness. It's intentional intensity, and it separates the elite from the average.

Reflection Question:

Where are you playing small or holding back? What does "Lion Mode" look like for you today?

_____

_____

_____

_____

_____

_____

_____

_____

Part 3
SUCCESS LEAVES CLUES

"The mind is the limit. As long as the mind can envision the fact that you can do something, you can do it."
– Arnold Schwarzenegger

KOBE BRYANT

MASTERING SELF-TALK

One of the most underrated tools in the mental game? **Self-talk.**

Nobody embodied this better than **Kobe Bryant.** His "Mamba Mentality" wasn't just about working harder—it was about controlling his mind through intentional, ruthless self-talk. Kobe once said, ***"I have self-doubt. I have insecurity. I have a fear of failure. But I don't capitulate to it. I harness it."***

He trained his inner voice like he trained his fadeaway—daily, with precision. During injury recovery, slumps, or the biggest moments of his career, Kobe talked to himself like a champion. He didn't wait for confidence to arrive—he created it through his words.

Self-talk isn't fluff. It's fuel. And it's **trainable.**

A fan-painted mural of Kobe Bryant in Santa Monica, CA.
Courtesy: PublicDomainImages.net

You can start right now—in the weight room, in the class-room, or before you take the field. When your heart's racing or you feel doubt creeping in, anchor yourself with a calm, clear phrase. When your brain starts yelling, *"What if?"* talk back with *"Let's go."*

Practical Ways to Build Elite Self-Talk:

- Create a **short mantra** you repeat before every rep (e.g., "I'm built for this" or "Next play").
- Catch and **replace negative thoughts** with truth (e.g., turn "I suck" into "I've trained for this").
- Say your **affirmations** out loud during warm-ups or in the mirror.
- Write **three power phrases** on your wrist tape, glove, notebook, or locker.

Key Takeaway:

You're always talking to yourself. Start controlling the conversation.

Reflection Question:

What's one phrase or mindset you can adopt this week to reset and bounce back when things go wrong?

_____

_____

_____

_____

_____

_____

_____

_____

_____

CRISTIANO RONALDO
VISUALIZATION AND POSITIVITY

One of the most powerful tools in your mental toolbox? **Visualization.**

Cristiano Ronaldo—one of the greatest athletes of all time—credits much of his success to his mind. He once said, *"I am always calm and relaxed before a match. I visualize the game—I see myself scoring, winning, celebrating."*

That's not superstition—it's science. **Ronaldo *trains his mind* like he trains his body**. He mentally rehearses free kicks, goals, celebrations, and pressure-packed moments. He's walked through success so many times in his head that when it happens in real life, it's familiar.

Your brain doesn't know the difference between a vividly imagined experience and a real one. That means every time you visualize success, you're stacking mental reps that translate to real confidence and sharper focus.

Cristiano Ronaldo in action during the season. *Courtesy @WONJONGSUNG on Pixabay*

You don't need to wait until game day to use this. Visualize in the locker room, in bed the night before, or right before practice. Get clear. Get specific. Feel it.

Practical Ways to Visualize Like Ronaldo:

- Before bed, close your eyes and **replay your perfect performance** in detail.
- **Use all of your senses** when visualizing—sight, sound, touch, smell, and emotion.
- During visualization, **see yourself overcoming adversity**, not just succeeding.

Key Takeaway:

If you can see it consistently, you can train yourself to believe it and achieve it.

Reflection Question:

What is one high-pressure moment you can start mentally rehearsing today?

_____

_____

_____

_____

_____

_____

_____

_____

_____

MOOKIE BETTS

CONFIDENCE UNDER PRESSURE

One of the most underrated traits of elite athletes? *Controlled confidence through preparation.*

Mookie Betts—World Series champion, MVP, and one of the most complete players in baseball—credits his *mental preparation* as the key to his success.

He once said in an interview:

"I just try to be consistent. Consistency comes from preparation—once I know I've done the work, I can relax and go play freely."

Mookie Betts with the Los Angeles Dodgers
in the outfield during a 2023 game at
Progressive Field in Cleveland
*by Erik Drost is licensed under CC
BY 2.0. Disclaimer: Use of this image
does not imply endorsement by the creator.*

That mindset is elite. Mookie isn't guessing when he steps in the box. He's *earned* his confidence through hours of physical and mental reps. He studies pitchers. He anticipates counts. He knows his plan. That level of intentionality removes fear. It builds belief. And it creates freedom to compete without hesitation.

When you prepare relentlessly, game day doesn't feel like pressure—it feels like *payoff*.

Practical Ways to Prepare Like Mookie:

- **Keep a journal:** Track your habits, workouts, and how you feel each day. Data builds awareness.
- **Watch the film:** Study pitchers or opponents. Know your plan before you step into the competition.
- **Simulate pressure:** Practice like it's game day. Rep your routine with intensity.
- **Decompress off the field:** Mookie golfs, bowls, and finds balance to keep a clear head.

Key Takeaway:

Confidence isn't random. It's earned. If you want to feel unshakable on game day, you have to put in intentional work behind the scenes.

Reflection Question:

What's one area of your game where you can prepare more intentionally this week?

_____

_____

_____

_____

_____

_____

_____

_____

_____

THE WALK-OFF

One of the biggest moments of my college career came when I wasn't even in the starting lineup.

It was a tie game against Ball State. Bottom of the ninth. Bases loaded. Two outs. Series on the line. My name got called to pinch hit, and in that moment, **everything slowed down**.

I stepped into the box calm, ready, confident. I trained for this. I earned this. First pitch: swung at a hanging breaking ball. *Walk-off hit*. Game over.

That one swing changed everything. It was more than a highlight—it was a reflection of all the extra reps, the mindset work, the visualizations, and the belief I had built brick by brick. I didn't get that opportunity by luck. I got it by owning my role and staying ready.

A fired-up TG after his pinch-hit walk-off vs. Ball State.
Credit: Oregon Athletics

Your role might change—starter, bench guy, pinch hitter, redshirt—but your **value** and **energy** never should. The most elite players are always prepared. They see every opportunity as their moment, and they **never** let doubt take over their mind.

Practical Ways to Apply This:

- **Embrace your current role** and commit to being the best at it.
- **Visualize succeeding in big moments**, even if they haven't come yet.
- **Stay ready** with daily routines that match your goals, not your current position.

Key Takeaway:

You don't need to start to make an impact. Great players stay ready—and deliver when it matters most.

Reflection Question:

If your number was called today, would you be ready—mentally, physically, emotionally?

_____

_____

_____

_____

_____

_____

_____

_____

_____

Part 4

PERSPECTIVE, GRATITUDE, AND GROWTH

"When you change the way you look at things,
the things you look at change."
– Wayne Dyer

GOOD: A MINDSET FOR LIFE

One of the most powerful mindset shifts I've ever come across comes from **Jocko Willink**, former Navy SEAL and best-selling author. His response to adversity is just one word:

"Good."

Didn't make the lineup? *Good—more time to work.*

Failed a test? *Good—now you know what to fix.*

Injured? *Good—now you'll strengthen other areas.*

This isn't fake positivity. It's not pretending everything is perfect. It's **extreme ownership**—the idea that *everything* is an opportunity to get better if you choose to see it that way.

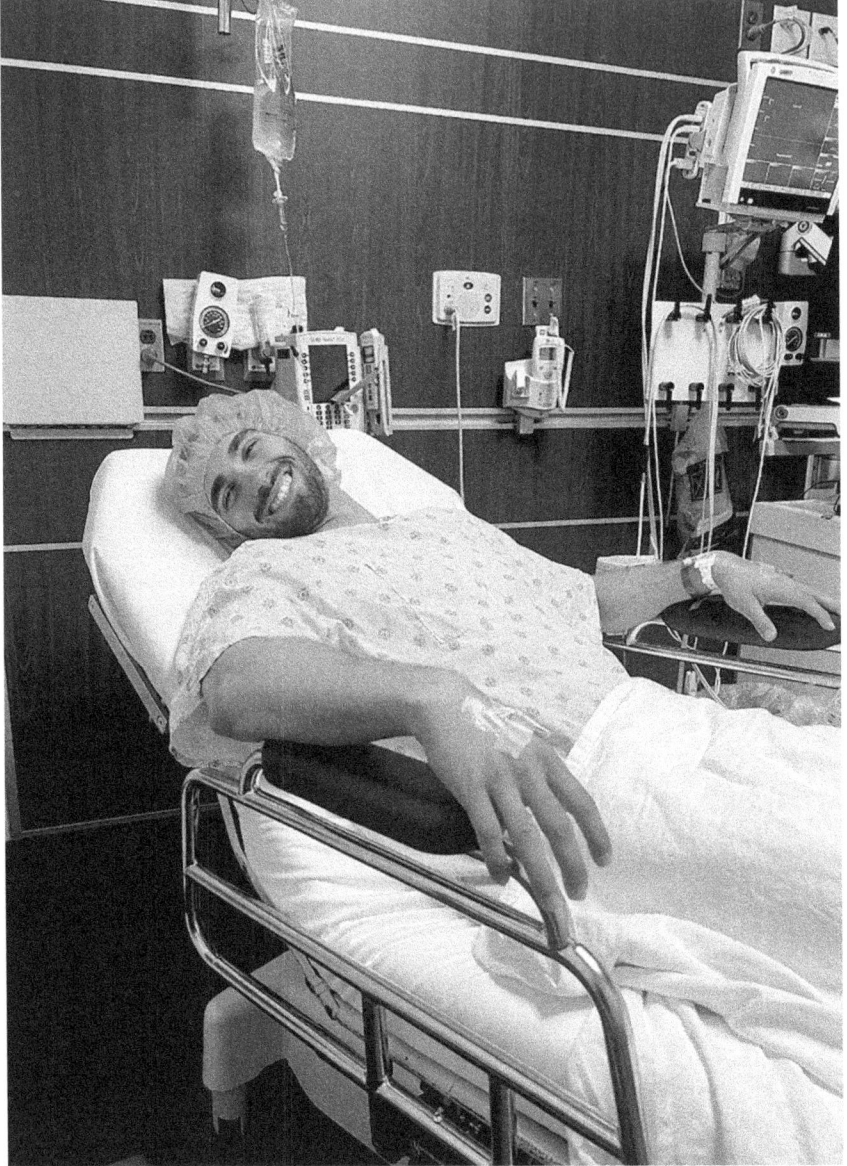

Tyler smiles before surgery to remove his hamate bone.

Jocko says that adversity is the test. Your response is the grade. When things don't go your way, how quickly can you shift from frustration to forward motion? Can you use setbacks as fuel? That's what separates the elite from the average—not just talent, but how they handle tough moments.

You won't always control the outcome. But you can always control your response.

Practical Ways to Apply the "Good" Mindset:

- When something goes wrong, pause and say **"Good"** out loud—then ask, "What can I do now?"
- **Journal daily** about one setback and what you gained from it.
- **Reframe failure as feedback**—start asking, *What is this teaching me?*
- Use **challenges as checkpoints**, not finish lines.

Key Takeaway:

Say "Good" to adversity. Let it sharpen you, not stop you.

Reflection Question:

What's one tough situation you can reframe right now as "Good"?

_____

_____

_____

_____

_____

_____

_____

_____

_____

_____

DODGER STADIUM TO WRIGLEY FIELD

Some baseball memories stay with you forever—not just because of *what* happened, but because of *where* they happened. I've had the honor of playing in some of the most historic stadiums in the world: **Dodger Stadium** during the CIF State Final in high school, and **Wrigley Field** while at Northwestern.

At Dodger Stadium, we (Harvard-Westlake) lost 2–0 in a hard-fought battle to Cypress. I was a high school kid playing where legends like Fernando Valenzuela, Clayton Kershaw, and Sandy Koufax had made history. The moment was bigger than the score.

Tyler [left], Sam Hliboki [middle], and Bennett Markinson [right] soak in the national anthem before the game.

At Wrigley, we walked off Ohio State with a 12–2 win (run-rule in 7 innings). I hit the hardest ball of the day (108.3 mph) and had a multi-hit game. The ivy walls, the huge Jumbotrons —it felt like magic. But what I remember most wasn't the stats. It was the feeling: **I was living a dream.**

In those moments, I remembered *why* I play—for the love of the game, for the one-on-one battles, for the chance to master something difficult, and for my friends and family who always had my back. Playing in those stadiums reminded me: **be grateful**, be present. Soak in every second.

Practical Ways to Apply This:

- Before each game, **take a moment to reflect** on what you're grateful for.
- Write down one thing each week that reminds you **why you play**.
- **Express appreciation** to your teammates, coaches, and family regularly.

Key Takeaway:

Gratitude keeps you grounded, especially when you're living the dream.

Reflection Question:

What's one moment in your journey that reminded you how lucky you are to play this game?

_____

_____

_____

_____

_____

_____

_____

_____

_____

ADVICE TO MY YOUNGER SELF

If I could go back and talk to my younger self, I wouldn't bring up stats, trophies, or highlight plays. I'd talk about *presence*.

I'd say, **"Slow down. Don't miss the magic of the moment."**

Enjoy the early morning lifts. Embrace the struggle of slumps. Laugh more in the dugout or on the sidelines. Breathe deeply before each pitch. Love your teammates harder. Stay grounded in your "why."

As you climb the ranks—from youth to high school, college, or even the professional level—the stakes get higher. So does the pressure. But the real secret to longevity? **Staying connected to your love for the game.**

A young Tyler meets Chicago White Sox legend,
Paul Konerko.

When it's all said and done, it won't be the stat lines you remember. It'll be the bus rides, the pregame rituals, the friendships, and the growth. The person you became through the process.

If I could leave my younger self with one message, it'd be this: ***"Stay present, stay grateful, and never lose your joy."***

Practical Ways to Stay Present and Play Free:

- Before each game, take **one deep breath** and remind yourself why you love to play.
- Keep a **gratitude journal**—write down three moments each week that made you smile.
- Visualize a **highlight reel** of your favorite plays before bed—remind yourself of your growth.
- Use **mantras** like "Have fun" or "Play free" in high-pressure moments.
- If doubt creeps in, **respond with action:** body language, self-talk, and effort.

Key Takeaway:

Stay grounded in gratitude. The journey is the reward.

Reflection Question:

What would you say to your younger self? How can you live that advice now?

_____

_____

_____

_____

_____

_____

_____

_____

_____

GRADES MATTER MORE THAN YOU THINK

Many athletes ask about the role grades play in the recruiting process. Here's the truth: **sometimes, your transcript can be the difference between getting recruited ... or getting passed up.**

Solid academics open *doors*—especially at the high school and college level. Coaches love players who are eligible, responsible, and driven, not just on the field, but in the classroom. And the higher your GPA and test scores, the more schools can afford to say *yes*.

But the value of education doesn't stop once you're in college.

Tyler, after graduating from the University of Oregon.

When I created Collegiate Mind Mastery, I was a graduate student at Northwestern—and it wasn't just my baseball journey that shaped the vision. My professors, administrators, classmates, and the alumni network played a massive role in building the foundation of the company.

Never underestimate your education. The habits and connections you build as a student-athlete will serve you long after the final out of your career.

Practical Ways to Win in the Classroom:

- Sit in the **front row or middle** of the room—eliminate distractions.
- **Meet with each teacher/professor** once—build a relationship and show effort.
- Schedule *"studying"* into your calendar (study, tutors, + homework blocks).
- Create a **post-class review habit**—five minutes to summarize key takeaways.
- Use the **same focus** you bring to the field in your schoolwork—preparation = performance.

Key Takeaway:

Be elite in every aspect of your life—especially when no one's watching.

Reflection Question:

Are you giving your academics the same effort and attention that you give to your sport?

_____

_____

_____

_____

_____

_____

_____

_____

_____

FINAL CHALLENGE

STEP INTO YOUR GREATNESS

This book isn't just here to inspire you—**it's a call to action.**

You've got one shot at this. One window to chase your greatness. And that window? It's shrinking every single day.

So here's the challenge: **Do something this week that your future self will thank you for.**

Whether it's setting your alarm thirty minutes earlier, journaling your goals, sending that message to a teammate, or choosing discipline when no one's watching—**take that step**.

You don't need the perfect plan. You just need to move.

Tyler celebrates with first base coach, Cody Jefferis,
after a hit at Wrigley Field.
Credit: Henry Frieman, Northwestern Athletics

Because momentum builds confidence. And confidence builds habits.

No more waiting. No more excuses. **You were made for more.**

Practical Ways to Take Action This Week:

- Write down **three goals** for this month, and post the list where you'll see it every day.
- **Turn off notifications** for one hour to improve focus.
- **Celebrate a small win** each day, no matter how minor.

Final Takeaway:

Your time is now. Don't wait for permission to become elite. Own it.

Final Reflection Question:

What does "greatness" look like for you? What's stopping you from starting right now?

_____

_____

_____

_____

_____

_____

_____

_____

_____

THE EXTRA MILE

*"The difference between ordinary and
extraordinary is that little extra."*
– Jimmy Johnson

BONUS REFLECTIONS

Additional Reflection Prompts

My Top Three Strengths as an Athlete

Write down three personal strengths and how they help your performance on and off the field.

_____

_____

_____

_____

_____

_____

My Biggest Mental Challenge

Identify your biggest mental or emotional barrier and brain-storm at least two ways to overcome it.

_____

_____

_____

_____

_____

_____

_____

_____

_____

_____

_____

My Daily Routine: What Works and What Needs Improvement

Reflect on your current habits and routines. What helps you perform at your best? What holds you back?

_____

_____

_____

_____

_____

_____

_____

_____

_____

_____

_____

Setting an Actionable Goal for the Next Thirty Days

Write down one specific goal related to your athletic or academic growth, and outline three action steps to achieve it.

_____

_____

_____

_____

_____

_____

_____

_____

_____

_____

_____

Who Inspires Me and Why?

List people who motivate you and what qualities or achievements of theirs you want to emulate.

_____

_____

_____

_____

_____

_____

_____

_____

_____

_____

_____

My Pregame Mindset Checklist

Write down the thoughts, routines, or habits that help you feel confident and locked in before a game.

_____

_____

_____

_____

_____

_____

_____

_____

_____

_____

_____

How I Respond to Failure

Reflect on the last time you failed or struggled. What was your initial response? What could a stronger, more intentional response look like next time?

_____

_____

_____

_____

_____

_____

_____

_____

_____

_____

_____

My Support System

List three people who consistently challenge, support, or encourage you, and one way you can show appreciation for each of them.

_____

_____

_____

_____

_____

_____

_____

_____

_____

_____

What "Success" Means to Me

Define what success looks and feels like in your own words.
How has that definition evolved?

_____

_____

_____

_____

_____

_____

_____

_____

_____

_____

_____

Habits of My Future Self

Picture yourself five years from now, living your dream. What three habits does that version of you do daily that you could start working on today?

_____

_____

_____

_____

_____

_____

_____

_____

_____

_____

_____

My Inner Voice in Pressure Moments

Write down two to three phrases you want to say to yourself in high-pressure moments. Keep them short, clear, and empowering.

_____

_____

_____

_____

_____

_____

_____

_____

_____

_____

_____

What I Can Control (And What I Can't)

Identify recent situations that caused stress or frustration. Which parts were within your control? How can you better respond next time?

_____

_____

_____

_____

_____

_____

_____

_____

_____

_____

My "Why" Statement

Dig deep and write out your personal "why" (why you train, why you compete, and why this journey matters to you).

_____

_____

_____

_____

_____

_____

_____

_____

_____

_____

Energy Givers vs. Energy Drainers

List the habits, people, or routines that give you energy and those that drain it. What's one shift you can make this week?

_____

_____

_____

_____

_____

_____

_____

_____

_____

_____

_____

The Three Traits I Want to Be Known For

What three words or traits do you want others to associate with you as an athlete and person? What daily actions back those up?

_____

_____

_____

_____

_____

_____

_____

_____

_____

_____

READY TO LEVEL UP?

If you've made it this far, it's clear—you're built differently. You're not just here to be inspired. You're here to take action, grow your mindset, and build a successful future.

But this book is just the beginning.

If you're ready to take the next step—to level up your routine, your habits, your confidence, and your life—we want to help you do it. Scan the QR code below to sign up for a **free 1-on-1 coaching call** with our team. No pressure. No catch. Just one conversation that could unlock your next breakthrough.

Our mission at **Collegiate Mind Mastery** is simple: to help the next generation of student-athletes dominate every-thing they do—in the classroom, on the field, and in life. If that sounds like you, then we want you in our circle.

- Scan the following QR code for a free coaching call!
- Follow us for daily content, tips, and mindset boosts:
- Instagram: @CollegiateMindMastery
- TikTok: @CollegiateMindMastery
- YouTube: @CollegiateMindMastery
- Website: https://collegiatemindmastery.com
- Newsletter: Collegiate Mind Mastery

In closing, never forget this:

The game is short. The window is now. And every day is your next rep.

No matter what you're doing today ...

Remember to COMPETE.

Scan the QR Code for a free one-on-one coaching call!

ABOUT THE AUTHOR

Tyler Ganus – Founder of Collegiate Mind Mastery

Tyler grew up in Los Angeles and represented Team USA at the 12U Pan American Games in Mazatlán, Mexico, where he pitched in two combined no-hitters and brought home a silver medal —a memory that helped shape his love for competition and team success.

He attended Harvard-Westlake High School and walked on to the baseball team at the University of Oregon, where he earned a spot on the 2023 Pac-12 Championship team and completed his undergraduate degree in just three years. Then, Tyler transferred to Northwestern University, where he earned his first Division I scholarship, became an everyday starter, and helped lead the program to its highest win percentage in the last twenty years.

His journey—marked by resilience, grit, and a deep belief in self—reflects the heart of **Collegiate Mind Mastery**, the mindset and leadership brand he created while pursuing graduate studies. Tyler holds dual graduate certificates in Sports Communication and Technology Entrepreneurship, and graduated *summa cum laude* (above a 4.0 GPA) from both Oregon and Northwestern.

Some of his proudest achievements include:

- 2023 Pac-12 Champion
- Team USA Silver Medalist
- 2023 Rawlings "Big Stick" Batting Title (.345)
- 2025 Big Ten Sportsmanship Award
- 2025 Allstate/NACDA Good Works Team Winner
- 2025 Jackie Robinson Community & Impact Award Nominee
- 2025 Academic All-District Team
- 2025 Academic All-Big 10 Team
- 2025 Pomeranz Family Willie the Wildcat Award
- 2023 Jaqua Award (Highest Student-Athlete GPA at Oregon)
- B.S. in Music
- 6-time Dean's List
- Graduate Certificates in Sports Communication & Tech Entrepreneurship

Through *Master Your Mind* and **Collegiate Mind Mastery**, Tyler is on a mission to equip the next generation of student-athletes with the tools, habits, and mindset needed to become their best—on and off the field.